Contents

Preface

Costume culture is part of human life and a symbol of civilization. The appearance and evolution of clothing are closely connected with the economy, politics, military affairs, ideology, culture, religion and customs of a people. Costumes not only fulfill a material purpose, they also reflect the stages of cultural development of the society in which they evolve.

Chinese costume started to take on its distinct characteristics in prehistoric times, and experienced changes in almost all dynasties over thousands of years. Each historical period distinguished itself from the rest, yet the costumes of each period were also subtly connected, borrowing and learning from one another and developing continuously generation after generation.

It was about 5,000 years ago, in the New Stone Age, when primitive man started to develop agriculture, that the art of weaving textiles into garments emerged. Man discarded the animal skins he had covered himself with previously, and began to wear clothing manufactured specially.

As the economy and culture developed, and living standards rose, the demand for stylish and even luxurious costumes grew.

In the stages of slave and feudal society in ancient China, there was a strict hierarchical system of the various classes in society. This was reflected in the clothing styles of the people, and the trend lasted, with modifications, right up until the 20th century. Starting with the emperor, the robes worn by the upper classes, including the officials, bore

12, nine, seven, five or three patterns, according to the rank of the wearer. These patterns included the sun, the moon, stars, mountains, dragons, pheasants, fire, algae, sacrificial vessels, rice, axes, and a pattern composed of two Chinese character gong, which means bow. Sun, moon, star and mountain patterns were reserved for the garments of the emperor, as was the dragon. In the Ming and Qing dynasties, civil officials wore robes embroidered with patterns of nine kinds of birds, each type signifying a certain rank; military officers were distinguished by nine kinds of beasts.

Costumes for officials and for the common people differed greatly in terms of material and color. Official costumes were decorated pure and bright colors, while those for commoners were plain and dull. Golden yellow was used exclusively for the emperor's robes, bearing dragon patterns. As for material, gauze and all kinds of silks and satins were reserved for the nobility, while commoners were only allowed to wear cotton cloth and hemp. It is said that the imperial concubine Lady Yang of the Tang Dynasty had 700 embroiderers and tailors for her exclusive use.

Traditional Chinese costumes came in various styles and forms, owing to political, ethnological and regional differences of each dynasty. The philosophical ideas of Confucianism and Taoism, as well as the esthetic standards of the feudal ethical code influenced clothing styles greatly. For instance, the ancient Chinese costumes followed the principle of strictly level and vertical lines, with plain and simple structure and parallel connection of parts. The front, back, body and sleeves are all connected to form an integrated whole, and to make the costume look elegant and the wearer generous and magnanimous – in much the same way as the artistic and cultural taste expressed by traditional Chinese freehand brushwork painting.

During the Warring States Period (475-221B.C.), marked by the emergence of various contending schools of thought, there was a great deal of experimentation in clothing. In the Wei, Jin, and Southern and Northern Dynasties period (220-581), the rise of metaphysics and the coming of Buddhism strongly influenced social and cultural life. People became more liberal and open-minded, which promoted the development of art and culture. Calligraphy became an independent art with the official and running scripts gradually forming their own free, natural and graceful styles. Clothing in this period is marked by long, flowing sleeves, reflecting the same easy, free and graceful style. In the Sui and Tang dynasties (581-907) China was a unified and prosperous country, and clothing became luxuriant. Liberal styles came to the fore, especially in women's garments, which were tailored to accentuate the lines of the body and even expose parts of it. With the ascendancy of the Confucian school of idealist philosophy in the Song (960-1279) and Ming (1368-1644) dynasties, there was a return to simple, natural and somewhat conservative clothing. The imperial court even ordered women to dress in simple and subdued garments. Extravagance in dress was strictly forbidden, even for court ladies. By the end of the Qing Dynasty (1644-1911), as Western culture was gradually introduced into China, people started to dress more for their own convenience.

There were several big reforms in ancient Chinese costumes, clearly influenced by the fashions of minority ethnic groups. At the same time, various ethnic minorities also absorbed much from the Han people's costumes, each supplementing and enriching the other during long periods of cultural exchanges. King Wuling of the State of Zhao in the Warring States Period ordered his troops to learn horse-riding and archery from the nomadic northwestern tribes. In the process, they adopted the short coats with narrow sleeves and a tight waist and boots which the tribesmen wore. This costume was more convenient for warfare than the traditional robes of the people of China's Central Plains. Han Dynasty (206B.C.-A.D.220) Emperor Wudi sent envoys twice to the western regions to open up trade and diplomatic relations with the kingdoms and tribes of Central Asia. It was not long before large quantities of silks were exported to the West, together with other aspects of Chinese culture, along the "Silk Road." From a Han Dynasty tomb in the Xinjiang Uygur Autonomous Region was excavated a well preserved silk robe. It is in typical ethnic minority style, yet the material and design are obviously Han. The endemic warfare during the Wei and Jin dynasties drove large numbers of northern ethnic minority people into the Central Plains, where their clothing fashions were adopted by the local Han inhabitants. The Sui and Tang dynasties were a period of great prosperity for the people of the Central Plains. Chang'an, the capital and the biggest city in the world at that time, attracted people of a huge number of nationalities, who came mainly to trade. Their influence on the Han women's clothing included exotic and gorgeous costumes, and the wearing of veils and heavy make-up. Some of the costumes were totally original, a quintessence of superbly combined costumes from different ethnic groups. The Liao, Jin, Yuan and Qing dynasties were actually founded by ethnic minorities, and so clothing in these periods was heavily influenced by the new ruling classes. For instance the Yuan Dynasty costumes were typically Mongolian, and the cheongsam, a closely fitting woman's dress with a high neck and slit skirt popular in the first half of the 20th century was developed from the typical Manchu woman's dress.

Despite the fact that the ancient Chinese costumes in each historical period had different characteristics, there was some continuity with regard to style, cut, design and color.

In terms of style, the two-piece costume (separate upper and lower garments) and one-piece gown type costume were adopted alternatively or sometimes simultaneously. The former was dominant until well into the Zhou Dynasty, when the one-piece garment first appeared, as the Spring and Autumn Period (770-476 B.C.) was succeeded by the Warring States Period. From the Sui and Tang dynasties on, women's dresses were mostly two-piece (jacket and skirt), while men's garments were mostly one-piece gowns.

In cut, narrow sleeves were in vogue under the influence of the costume of the Hu tribes of north and west China, prior to the Sui Dynasty. Women's clothing consisted of a close-fitting upper garment and a puffed-out skirt. In the Song Dynasty, the typical woman's upper garment became longer, while the lower garments became shorter, with most women wearing ankle-length pleated skirts.

As far as pattern designs are concerned, the sequence was solid – magnificent – natural – heavy and complicated. In the earliest dynasties – those of the Shang and Zhou – clothing decoration patterns were simple. Later, orderly composition was stressed, and in the Ming and Qing dynasties the designs gradually became more exquisite and refined.

Clothing colors in ancient times tended to be simple and bright. Later, complicated and carefully-matched colors were widely used, such as red and yellow, yellow and green, and green and blue.

The long history of Chinese costumes is a great story of the development of a creative art. In the process of evolution of the styles of garments of the Chinese nation, convergence and divergence have always existed side by side, and the special contribution they have made to the world cultural tradition is being more and more appreciated.

According to historical records, the official costumes of the Chinese emperors took shape during the Western Zhou Dynasty (11th century B.C.-771B.C.). The clothing and adornment of the emperors of ancient China were composed of the official crowns and costumes, the distinctive 12 symbolic patterns and images (the sun, the moon, stars, mountains, dragons, pheasants, fire, algae, sacrificial vessels, rice, axes, and a pattern composed of two Chinese character gong, which means bow.) The loose-fitting, bright yellow garments, headgear and patterns were exclusive to the emperors, symbolizing the highest power.

The official costume of an emperor of the Han Dynasty (206B.C.-A.D.220) bears the 12 patterns exclusive to the emperor. The number of the patterns on clothing shrank progressively with the descending scale of rank. After the Qin Dynasty, yellow was the favorite color for the emperors' robes down until the end of feudal rule in 1911. ▼

▲ The official costumes of an emperor of the Qin Dynasty (221-206B.C.) are loose. Strings of pearls dangle from a crown, which veiled his face. The shoes were broad and sturdy. Black was the favorite color during the Qin Dynasty.

Crown and square,
wing-headed shoes
of an emperor of the
Han Dynasty

The imperial robe of Li Shimin,
the second emperor of the Tang
Dynasty (618-907)

An empress of the Song Dynasty (960-1279) wearing a ceremonial robe and pearl-adorned phoenix coronet, and palace maids with gorgeous hats. Phoenix symbols were common on the clothing and ornaments of empresses and imperial concubines.

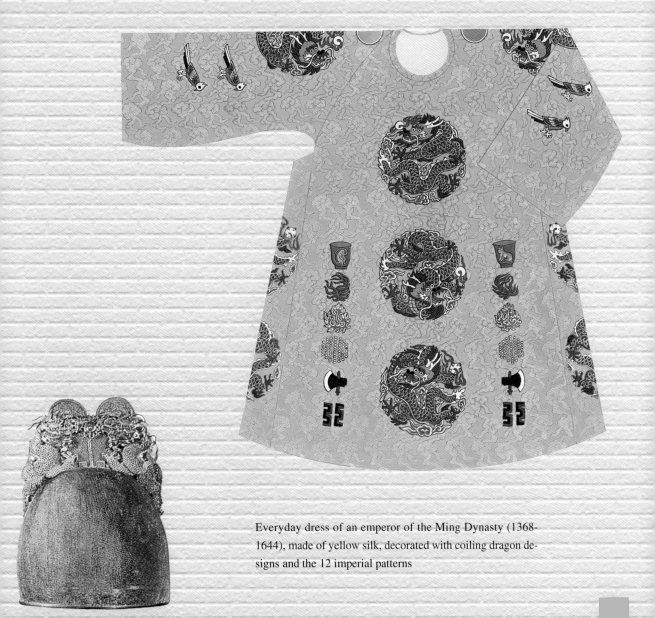

Everyday dress of an emperor of the Ming Dynasty (1368-
1644), made of yellow silk, decorated with coiling dragon designs and the 12 imperial patterns

Phoenix coronet made with pearls and jade,
as worn by the empress and imperial concubines of Emperor Wanli of the Ming Dynasty

Crown decorated with gold wire of a
Ming emperor

Clothing and ornaments of Empress Dowager Cixi, who ruled behind the scenes during emperors Tongzhi and Guangxu's reign periods of the Qing Dynasty (1644-1911). The Qing empresses and imperial concubines wore clothes characterized by the distinctive features of the women's dress of the Manchu ethnic group—the high-necked cheongsam, "flowerpot" shoes, and winged headdress.

Colorful dress worn by an empress or imperial concubine of the Qing Dynasty

Court dress, crown and boots of a Qing emperor, decorated with rare fur in autumn and winter, and satin in spring and summer

Court gown of the Yongzheng reign period of the Qing Dynasty, decorated with embroidered dragons

Gorgeous robe of Wan
Rong, concubine of the
last emperor of the Qing
Dynasty

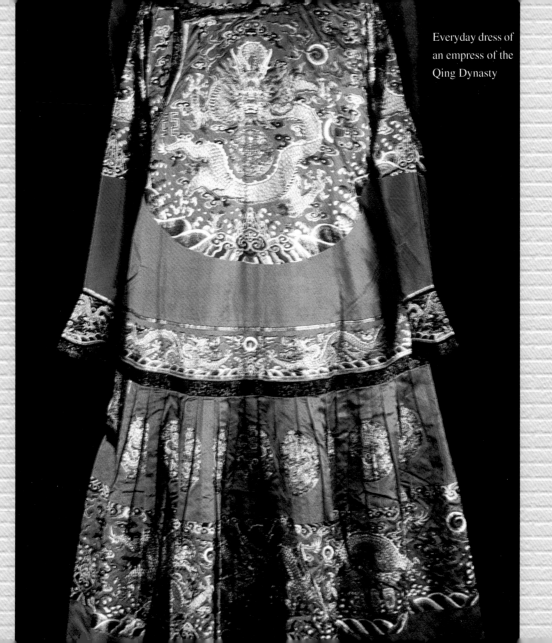

Everyday dress of
an empress of the
Qing Dynasty

Wraps of the Qing Dynasty, to be worn outside
the robe of an empress or imperial concubine, decorated with pearl embroidery and tassels

Government Officials' Clothing

Traditionally, there were
nine grades of official rank. Before the Ming
Dynasty, the official ranks were differentiated by the
number of the 12 patterns (see previous section) on the robes
– in descending order. Officials wore soft hats before the Tang
Dynasty, and hard ones afterwards. A Song Dynasty emperor made
the projecting wings on the hats longer and straight so as to prevent the
officials putting their heads together and whispering during court sessions.
The ceremonial gowns worn by government officials of the Ming and
Qing dynasties bore a square embroidered patch on the breast and back,
respectively. The patterns of the patches distinguished the status and ranks
of the civil and military officials. The gowns of the civil officials were
decorated with birds such as red-crowned cranes and golden pheasants;
and the military officials wore patches with representations of fierce
animals such as lions, tigers and leopards. Hats also served to
differentiate the official ranks by means of pearl buttons
on the top, peacock feathers and red tassels.

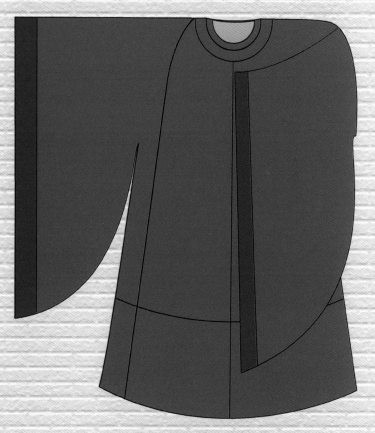

Wide-sleeved blouse, jade
belt and winged hat – Song
Dynasty official uniform

A robe, black gauze cap and ceremonial gown worn by a Ming government official

Buzi, a square embroidered patch on the breast and back of the robe of a first-grade government official of the Qing Dynasty ▲

Gown of a civilian official of the Qing Dynasty

Summer (top) and winter (bottom)hats of Qing government officials

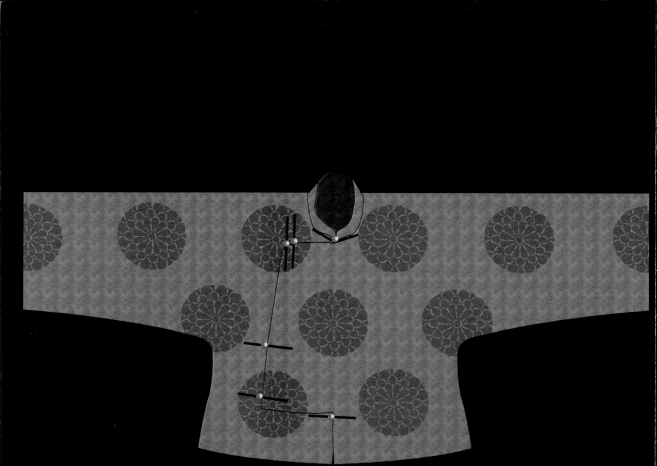

Satin-faced embroidered every-day clothes of Qing government officials. The crane and sunrise pattern represents auspiciousness.

Warriors' Dress

During the Warring States Period (475B.C.-221B.C.), King Wuling of the State of Zhao reformed the outfits of his soldiers. This marked a departure from the wearing of broad-sleeved gowns on the battlefield. From then on, soldiers wore jackets with narrow sleeves, trousers and boots, over which they donned armor.

Armor of the Qin Dynasty consisted of pieces of iron or leather protecting the shoulders, chest and abdomen. The plates, which come in the shape of squares, rectangles, fish scales or tortoise shells, were jointed together with iron nails for more convenient movement.

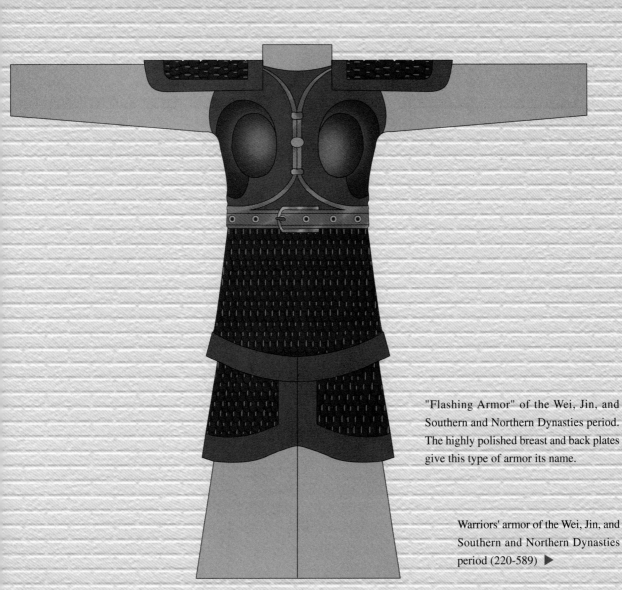

"Flashing Armor" of the Wei, Jin, and Southern and Northern Dynasties period. The highly polished breast and back plates give this type of armor its name.

Warriors' armor of the Wei, Jin, and Southern and Northern Dynasties period (220-589) ▶

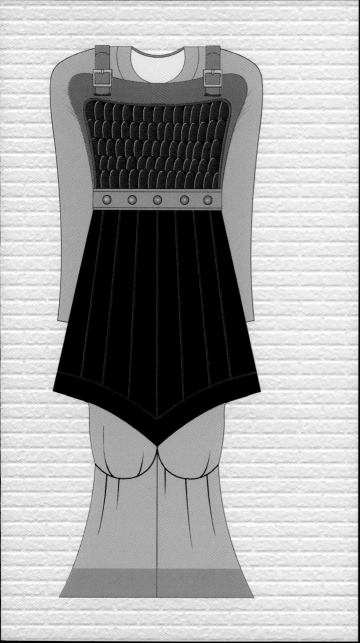

The ornateness of this complete set of soldier's armor, helmet and boots reflects the prosperity of the mid-Tang Dynasty, when the empire was powerful and at peace. In addition to iron and leather armor, guards of honor wore suits of thin armor stitched onto tough silk. Even paper armor was used on some ceremonial occasions.

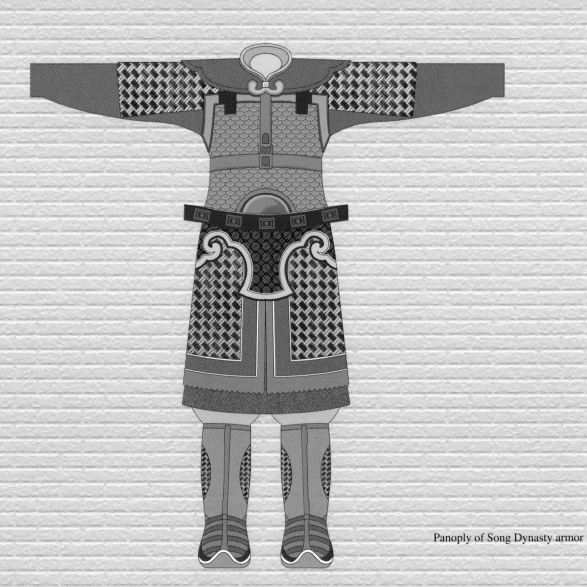

Panoply of Song Dynasty armor

Battledress of Mongolian cavalry of
the Yuan Dynasty (1279-1368)

Armor of high-ranking military
officers of the Ming Dynasty

Dress of a military officer of the Qing Dynasty. The helmet is made of silk fabric, and the armor is decorated with copper nails. The detachable collar, neckplate and helmet earflaps are embroidered with patterns. Except for two metal plates to protect the chest and the back, the dress has no plates. ▼

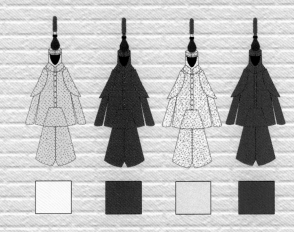

Battle gear of Manchu soldiers of the Qing Dynasty

Clothing of the Upper Classes

The upper classes in the olden days included government officials, landowners and wealthy merchants and some scholars. Their garments are usually painstakingly made of the finest materials and often richly decorated. The difference between costumes of the upper class and those of the common folks is particularly notable in women's clothing – in the design of collars and dress.

Clothing and accessories said to have belonged to Confucius, China's most famous philosopher and educator

Typical garments of the Warring States Period . This
era marked a dramatic change in Chinese clothing
styles – from basic and simple to ornate and
ostentatious.

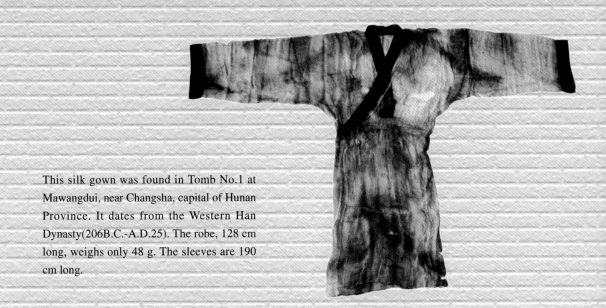

This silk gown was found in Tomb No.1 at Mawangdui, near Changsha, capital of Hunan Province. It dates from the Western Han Dynasty(206B.C.-A.D.25). The robe, 128 cm long, weighs only 48 g. The sleeves are 190 cm long.

Cotton print gown with crimson gauze front, also found in Tomb No. 1 at Mawangdui. The gown is 130 cm long and the sleeves are 236 cm long. The style of dress of the aristocrats of the Han Dynasty was simple and dignified. The most common materials were brocade and silk with base patterns, and the overall color was light, showing an unsophisticated simplicity.

Lady with double hair buns in the painting *Goddess of the Luo River*

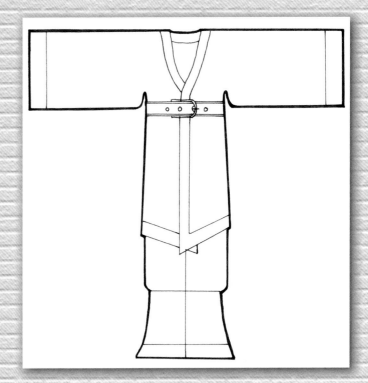

Lady of the Northern and Southern
Dynasties period with upright hair
buns and shoes with curling edges

Clothing and accessories of the Northern and
Southern Dynasties

Women's dress of
the Tang Dynasty

Ladies of the Tang Dynasty wearing long skirts, short embroidered capes and high hair buns. Both wide and narrow sleeves were in fashion, so were shoes with curling edges. The clothes were commonly made of silk and satin with myriad patterns.

Aristocratic women wearing broad-sleeved gauze garments, long skirts and short embroidered capes in the painting *Court Ladies Wearing Flowered Head-dresses of the Tang Dynasty*, by Zhou Fang. This painting depicts aristocratic women strolling in a courtyard. The women were dressed exotically. For example, they wore big flowers in their hair, and see-through dresses. Silk and gauze were commonly used as materials for women's clothes in the Tang Dynasty. Covering the body with gauze and not wearing underwear was unprecedented and was a reflection of the liberal atmosphere of the society of that era.

Another close-up from the *Court Ladies Wearing Flowered Headdresses*. The clothing of the Tang and Song dynasties is characterized by symmetrical and neat decorative patterns.

A noblewoman, from the painting *Court Ladies Wear-ing Flowered Headdresses*

Aristocratic woman and
her female attendants, from
a mural at the Dunhuang
Grottoes, Tang Dynasty

Tang Dynasty noblewoman

Tang Dynasty noblewoman

Tang Dynasty noblewoman

A noblewoman of the
Tang Dynasty

Wealthy man and his
servants, Tang Dynasty
(Dunhuang murals)

A noblewoman of the Tang
Dynasty, with fashionable
high hair buns

Shoes of the Tang Dynasty

Headdresses of noblewomen of
the Tang Dynasty

Headdresses of young girls
of the Tang Dynasty

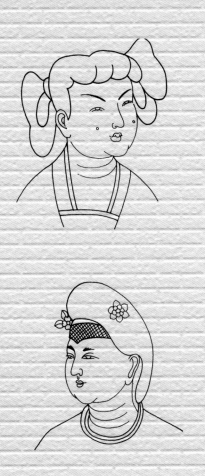

Headdresses of noblewomen
of the Tang Dynasty

Young noblewomen of the Tang Dynasty,
with fashionable flower cheek patches

Noblewomen wearing the latest fashions in the picture *Revelry of the Wealthy of the Tang Dynasty*

Clothing of aristocratic men and women of the Five Dynasties period (part of the painting *The Night Revels of Han Xizai*). The artist sneaked into the party, and later recreated the scene from memory. The people, costumes and utensils are realistically depicted and accurately reflect the life of the Five Dynasties period.

Dress of scholars of the Song Dynasty

Blouse with a straight collar, typical woman's dress
of the Song Dynasty

"Paddy field clothes" of the Ming Dynasty, made of odd scraps of cloth patched together. Such garments were popular among the women of the Ming and Qing dynasties.

Aristocratic women of the Ming Dynasty dressing and making up. The patterns and designs on clothes in the Ming and Qing dynasties were mostly realistic depictions.

Hair ornaments of noblewomen of
the Ming Dynasty

Aristocratic women of the Ming Dynasty at home

Bijia—sleeveless long clothes popular among lower-class women of the Ming Dynasty

A noblewoman of the Qing Dynasty. Women's clothing and ornaments of the Qing Dynasty are characterized by the narrow-sleeved cheongsam, the front of which buttons on the left, the winged headdress called *dalachi* and "flowerpot" shoes. Women's dresses of the Qing Dynasty, different from those of other dynasties, have inlaid embroidery on the hems.

Everyday dress of
noblewomen of
the Qing Dynasty

Clothing and ornaments of
three noblewomen of the Qing
Dynasty

Clothing and ornaments of
a noblewoman of the Qing
Dynasty

Manchu women's dress of the
Qing Dynasty

Three styles of women's sleeveless jackets
of the Qing Dynasty

Small embroidered bags used as ornaments by noblewomen of the Qing Dynasty

Embroidered bags containing folding fans of noblewomen of the Qing Dynasty

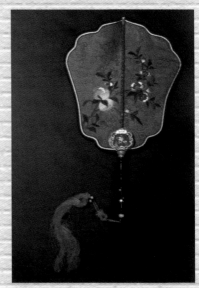

Four types of circular fans used by noblewomen of the Qing Dynasty

Dresses of noblewomen of the Kangxi reign period
(1662-1722) of the Qing Dynasty

Clothing and ornaments of aristocratic men and women of the Qianlong reign period (1736-1795) of the Qing Dynasty

Clothing and ornaments of aristocratic women of the
Yongzheng reign period (1723-1735) of the Qing Dynasty

Stage costumes of Bai Niangzi and Xiao Qing in the opera *Flooding the Golden Hill*, Qing Dynasty

Broad-sleeved gown edged with lace, and leggings of the Qing Dynasty

Clothing of the Common People

The common people in ancient China included slaves, serfs, servants and clerks. Their clothing, naturally, consisted of basic garments, and even their best clothes had no hint of extravagance. The sleeves of their jackets were narrow, not wide like those of rich people and the aristocracy, and their shoes and hats were coarsely made.

An everyday scene of the common people – talking

From the murals about the working people of the Wei, Jin and Northern and Southern Dynasties period we can see that the clothes of the peasants cultivating fields and hunting, and of women baking pancakes and steaming buns consist of simple, open-neck jackets tied around the waist.

Clerks riding horses, Wei and Jin dynasties

Setting out for the fields,
Wei and Jin dynasties

Ploughing the field, Wei and
Jin dynasties

Winnowing, Wei and
Jin dynasties

Playing musical
instruments, Wei
and Jin dynasties

Carrying water, Wei
and Jin dynasties

Baking pancakes, Wei
and Jin dynasties

Steaming buns, Wei and Jin dynasties

Hunting, Wei and Jin dynasties

Grazing sheep, Wei and Jin dynasties

Pasturing horses, Wei and Jin dynasties

Peasant woman winnowing, wearing
an open-neck dress, Sui Dynasty

A lower-class woman of the Tang Dynasty. Notice the elbow-length sleeves.

A mounted imperial bodyguard of the
Tang Dynasty, wearing a tunic showing
the influence of the western tribes people

Imperial bodyguards of
the Tang Dynasty

Imperial palace maids of the Tang Dynasty wore padded clothes, skirts, capes and narrow-sleeved dresses, (from the painting *Ladies Preparing Newly Woven Silk* by Zhang Xuan).

Detail of the painting *Ladies Preparing Newly Woven Silk* by Zhang Xuan. Notice the narrow sleeves of their dress, obviously showing the influence of the ethnic minorities in western China.

Women of the Tang Dynasty wearing clothes influenced by the styles of the western ethnic minorities

Clothing and ornaments of female musicians of the Five Dynasties period (detail of the painting *The Night Revels of Han Xizai*)

A common woman of
the Song Dynasty

Working women of the Song Dynasty. The images are taken from brick carvings of that period.

A groom's tunic, Song Dynasty

Song Dynasty tea merchants wearing the
typical straw sandals of the common
people of those days

Costumes of (from top, clockwise)
a peddler, knife grinder and fortune
teller of the Yuan Dynasty

A blind man of the Yuan Dynasty

Uniforms of imperial bodyguards of the Yuan Dynasty

Clothing and accessories of a preg-
nant woman of the Yuan Dynasty ▼

◀ Stage costumes of *zaju* opera
performers of the Yuan Dynasty

Clothing and ornaments of four pro-
fessional female palace singers of
the Ming Dynasty

There was a great change in Chinese women's hair styles from the early Qing Dynasty to the initial period of the Republic of China, indicating a series of drastic social changes.

Dress designs by Ye Qianyu, an artist of the Republic of China period (1911-1949), for women in the post-feudal era. In this period, Chinese women were influenced by Japanese women's dresses and hair styles, both of which tended to be simple.

Red jackets with patched decorations were very popular during the period of the Republic of China.

◄ Combining a sleeveless jacket with a cheongsam was fashionable for a while during the period of the Republic of China.

Cheongsam design of the
Republic of China period

Appendix:

Evolution of Clothing and Accessories Throughout Chinese History

Dynasties	Western Zhou Dynasty (11th century B.C.-771B.C.)	Eastern Zhou Dynasty(770B.C.-256B.C.)	Qin Dynasty (221B.C.-206B.C.)	Han Dynasty (206B.C.-A.D.220)	Wei and Jin dynasties (220-420)	Northern and Southern dynasties (420-589)
Men's dress						
Women's dress						

图书在版编目（CIP）数据

中国传统服饰 / 袁杰英主编．－北京：外文出版社，2002.9
（中华风物）

ISBN 7-119-03058-2

I. 中... II. 袁... III. 服饰－简介－中国－英文
IV. TS941.742

中国版本图书馆 CIP 数据核字（2002）第 026221 号

"中华风物"编辑委员会

顾　　问：蔡名照　赵常谦　黄友义　刘质彬
主　　编：肖晓明
编　　委：肖晓明　李振国　田　辉　呼宝珉
　　　　　房永明　胡开敏　崔黎丽　兰佩瑾

责任编辑：杨春燕
英文翻译：顾文同　郁　苓
英文审定：贺　军
图　　片：袁杰英　席恒青
内文设计：席恒青
封面设计：席恒青

（本书部分图片得到上海市戏曲学校相助，
特此鸣谢。）

中国传统服饰

袁杰英 主编

Ⓒ 外文出版社

外文出版社出版
（中国北京百万庄大街 24 号）
邮政编码：100037
外文出版社网页：http://www.flp.com.cn
外文出版社电子邮件地址：info@flp.com.cn
sales@flp.com.cn
外文出版社照排中心制作
北京京都六环印刷厂印刷
中国国际图书贸易总公司发行
（中国北京车公庄西路 35 号）
北京邮政信箱第 399 号 邮政编码 100044
2002 年(24 开)第 1 版
2005 年第 1 版第 2 次印刷
（英文）
ISBN 7-119-03058-2/J・1589(外)
05800(平)
85-E-534 S

| Sui Dynasty (581-618) | Tang Dynasty (618-907) | Liao Dynasty (907-1125) | Song Dynasty (960-1279) | Yuan Dynasty (1279-1368) | Ming Dynasty (1368-1644) | Qing Dynasty (1644-1911) | Mordern Times (1911-1949) |

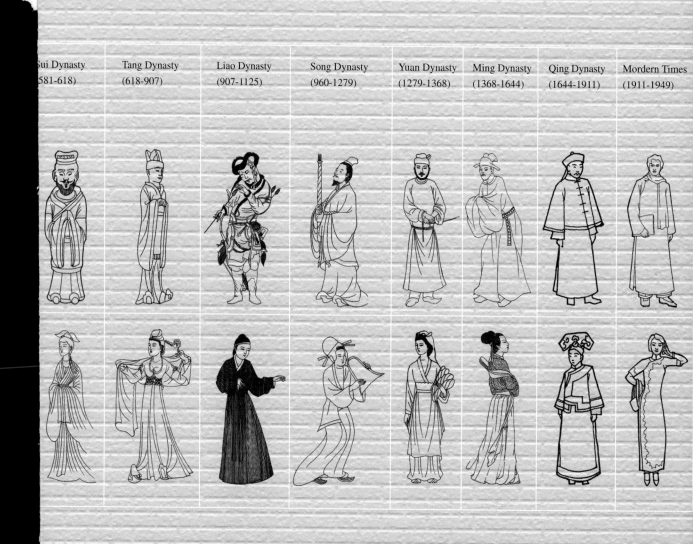